Bye Bye Blackbird

Doreen Stock

A Publication of The Poetry Box ®

Poems ©2021 Doreen Stock
All rights reserved.

Editing & Book Design: Shawn Aveningo Sanders
Cover Photograph: "Sophie at the Piano" by Amy Stock Drozd
Cover Illustration & Design: Robert R. Sanders
Author Photo: "Doreen at Annetta's Birthday" by Marcelo Holot

No part of this book may be reproduced in any manner whatsoever without permission from the author, except in the case of brief quotations embodied in critical essays, reviews and articles.

ISBN: 978-1-948461-81-8
Printed in the United States of America.
Wholesale Distribution via Ingram.

Published by The Poetry Box®, 2021
Portland, Oregon
ThePoetryBox.com

for Annetta Diamond Winnick
1918–2012

"A balanced mind
does not weigh
incorrectly"

is what was written
in your high school
annual of the beautiful
serious young woman
who stared out of its pages

Brilliance is what lasts,
Mother, polished by these
years of loving and being
loved

And strength. "How were
You brave enough to do that?"
I am often asked. Always
there is your firm voice echoing
in my heart, calming fears,
pointing me in new directions.

Those who ask that question
have never known you.

Contents

Bedouins Can Find Their Mothers	7
The Seal Report	8
The Angel of Sainte Chapelle	10
Feeding Mother in the Storm	12
Mother Horse	13
Clair de Lune	14
My Mother Flying Home	15
The Poem Geronimo	16
X-ray Tango	17
Orchards, Highway 5	18
Your Unbecoming	19
On the Dumping of Pianos	20
My Mom as Dylan Thomas	22
The Roadrunner	23
Bye Bye Blackbird	24
The Butterfly Blouse	25
Acknowledgments	27
Praise for *Bye Bye Blackbird*	29
About the Author	31

Bedouins Can Find Their Mothers

Arad, Israel, 1998

Bedouins can find
their mothers

there are signs
that only a daughter
can read

in the smallest portion
of the eyes
above the blackness

in the position
of even three rocks
on the slope at noon

there is a scent
of flowers that
were trampled and
bent

like the shadow of
a spine broken and
then re-formed
that the Bedouin
daughter can read

The Seal Report

It took a long walk in the pink air to put us back
together again. We had just hugged when we came
across her, small seal out of the sunset sea huddled
on the edge

Staring, breathing, suffering.

Two grown men needed to be photographed with her
one standing on each side of her head   the flash
of the camera exploding into her face as they smiled.

She seemed to be saying, "I can't do this anymore,"
telegraphing with her soft eyes, "I'm weak, I'm hungry,
I can't compete," as behind her two giant pelicans dove,
beaks down into the shimmering feed, and four or five
of her cousins performed a wet ballet, leaping so high off
the horizon I thought they were porpoises holding their flippers
out behind themselves like tails. She almost sighed, then moved
one part of her tailbone slightly to leave a strange imprint
in the darkening sand, tiny red light breaking behind one of her eyes.

I blew my top when we got home.
You stood there mutely, not at all understanding the report
I was trying to give. I wept large round tears.

The seal tried to return to the sea. I learned this. But couldn't make it
and came back to be guided with herding boards and a net into
a rubber-coated cage. They say hundreds of seals are starving this
summer, but they don't know why...

Hang on. I have to get the phone. Oh, that was my mother, she's bed-ridden, hardly can make it to the bathroom anymore and she was saying that the strange boat anchored just outside my window belongs to a billionaire from Montana. He has a helicopter on board and everything. Lots of brightly lit parties out there every night. Her cell phone cuts on and off so I can just barely get her voice, like someone from another world trying to tell me what's before my very eyes today. "Just thought I'd call to tell you what's what," crackle, click, said my mother's voice fading in and out, "Since you say you don't take the local papers anymore."

The Angel of Sainte Chapelle

When I first saw the Angel of Sainte Chapelle
"Oh my God he looks like my mother's doctor
at the rehab hospital, I shall have to rethink things,"
I thought, rethinking things, going back to the serious moment,
he seated at the foot of her bed, she having been transported (and this
is a verb we do not use lightly) from the trauma ward with her cracked
ischium and her cracked pubic bone to this space where, pink-curtained
off from her roommate who at the moment was eating fish and chips
with a laughing friend, she faced him, the doctor-angel-look-alike
as he said after a few, very few, I thought, preliminaries, "In the event
of a heart event, do you wish to be resuscitated?" And she looked

uncomprehendingly, I thought, but now I think she was staring
incredulously at those tall up and down wings of his chopped off
at the tippy top as if with a giant pruning shears as she said
in a faraway slightly confused voice unlike her usual commanding one,
"No."

No? My sister standing opposite shot me a pure blue look.
"I've had enough," Mother said, three plus days after tripping
in her internist's office, hitting her head on the toilet seat as she went
down, spilling her urine sample, her heavy braced foot shooting out
from under her, the aluminum walker standing there at the sink
without her, and then banging with her hand on said toilet seat
and calling out for help until finally being lifted into a chair, of all things,
by the internist himself, and just now being claimed as well by a raging
bladder infection requiring catheterization.

That angel filled out the shocking-pink form with a blue ballpoint pen,
putting an X in the little box next to the words, Do Not Resuscitate.

It was made clear to us at the museum that the backdrop in this photo
was a single white sheet, so the French photographer could capture
the angel's facial features as well as his stone robes and carved flying
things.

There was some sort of tight band about the head of the Angel of Sainte Chapelle. I wondered at the time what that was about, but now, after thinking it through, I think I understand the feeling.

Feeding Mother in the Storm

I push the wheelchair through strange hallways until it's time to make lunch for them all, my brother, my sister, and her, whose face I kiss, whose body I hug and unceremoniously plop onto a waiting bed. The cupboards are full of thick pink retro-glasses but nothing resembling a plate, plates being the problem in this dream, also dessert is a problem...

What I finally take for the sandwiches, hastily made, are used TV dinner foil flats cut on the diagonal so that each sandwich is served on a bumpy triangle.

"What's for dessert?" I am asked, and still rummaging for fruit, I wake up with a headache this morning to thunder and lightning, pounding surf, rain.

Mother Horse

Long ago when mothers were horses
with their big hearts against our small heads
we were calm next to their giant bodies and nothing
was too hard for them to do. They could lift us onto
their backs and run into the night sky never ever leaving
us behind, long ago, when we could feel them around us,
and they would bend their heads down to drink of still waters
and we were warm and safe.

Then came a time like *Guernica*. And they were terrified and white
with anguish, their big blue teeth bared in tragic ways, their necks
arched to the breaking point by the cruel harnesses of pain.

And then we were forced to lead separate lives. And we longed for
them as they streaked through our dream. They roamed the worlds
in search of us, and we could hear them whinnying across the abyss
of ice and black water that we would have to cross if ever we were
to find them again.

Clair de Lune

She is last to play in a field of ten, three judges tabled before the baby grand piano, and, past the immediate curtain of pure tension, hanging ivy is moving against the wall of windows through which can be seen, far-off, a man calmly seated on a stone ledge, his back to us and facing an expanse of the light-soaked San Francisco Bay.

She executes a crisp bow in black suit and floral tie, cuffs rolled back over jacket sleeves, presenting her small hands to the gleaming keys. A moment of silence to connect with the spirit of the composer, a sharp intake of breath, a whispered "Now!" and Claude Debussy fills the room, presses against the church windows, the rustling leaves fluttering against them, beyond the wide water, trembling. My mother, who has been gone five years now, soars into the room in cream flannel, coral roses on wings of a moonlit sadness, the music now pouring out of the black instrument at the touch of her great-granddaughter's hands.

The man begins to levitate slightly off the wall of stones, the water before him crashing in green waves against an invisible shore. There is perfume in the air, a far-away look as the sapphire eyes of the piano player search the invisible shore, the gleaming shore, threshold, majesty, a small golden crown settling onto her short blonde hair as Great-grandmother circles, circles above her in the moonlight, cream flannel, coral roses, and slowly vanishes. The man is high over the water now. He lifts one hand, palm open toward the glittering light-soaked bay above which a blue moon has slowly risen! Ah! His favorite perfume, and we can smell it…

My Mother Flying Home

Not the person anyone can see
in long gown of lavender lace
my Mother is flying over the clouds

Not the embarrassed-in-green-pantsuit
ninety-year-old wheeled down the aisle
before a full planeload of watching eyes
hands crossed over chest in victim position

She sails trailing rippling skirts, one blue foot
dangling in air, face calm, majestic,
white hair fluffy, piled high,
my Mother accompanied by a silent
music is winging over Iceland and Greenland,
over the snow-capped planet…

Not the one grabbing on hard to the airliner bathroom
sink, so hard the hand bones wince, not she dragging
her braced foot over the threshold, not the one
trying to manage a turn in that cramped space,
with me guarding her progress before closeting her in
with the folding door

My Mother in long gown
of lavender lace is gliding through air lanes,
atoms of light dancing through her, remote,
sly, on the wing, away from it all, withdrawing
from her pocket amid folds of anemone froth
one perfect chocolate and resting her elbow
on a platform of billowing blue is eating it, ecstatic,
not the person anyone at all can see, she soars
swimmingly all the way from Paris that City of Light
homeward to her little rose-colored bed

to sleep…

The Poem Geronimo

Is written at seventy miles per hour with second driver
up front and he (yes, that's really his name, Geronimo)
black hair combed smoothly back from his brow
(think: crow's wing in the wind here) bends over
my mother in the ambulance to change her diaper, returning
her home from the hospitals of the north to die in the desert,
her own bit of heaven: couch by the TV, bed by the white-
curtained window, rabbits under the yellow lounge chairs,
a glimpse of the orange tree, laden, through the patio window.

She can see me reading in the living room under the yellow
rain of the lamp in my favorite chair,
I can see her reading in her bed by the yellow
rain of the lamplight...

The poem Geronimo is written at seventy miles per hour and he
answers (think: the essence of upright kindness here) "I've got
babies, I'm used to diapers!") to her questioning look,
speeding past almond orchards in full bloom...
Is this really happening to me, and this young man
with the movie star face is changing my diaper?

At seventy miles per hour without losing balance, without bumping
his head on the overhanging glass full of life-saving equipment.
At seventy, without losing humane dignity, rolling the 93-year-old
patient back and forth as the job demands and then, 10 minutes later,
as the infected bladder squirts, returning with a joke and a smile to do
it again (think: angel here, a term I do not use lightly) asking me
meanwhile if I'm OK as we speed past the hawk poised on its
fence post listening, listening in the crosswinds of the cars to
swoop down on the little rustling being under the grass and take her
while the light of love shines out of the eyes of all of us...

Geronimo.

X-ray Tango

Good, I wore the new track shoes with orthopedic inserts, ugly things, but the better to steady my partner within our embrace before the El Mirador Medical Center X-ray machine, she, scared shitless without her walker, me, in the leaded vest provided. "Steady now, a few more minutes," yelled the tech from his booth.

I had her under the arm, said track shoes firmly planted, holding my only mom while somewhere the crisp wild carrot leaf curled on the road to the contagious hospital, in her 92nd spring.

Orchards, Highway 5

I so far, moving farther from your grave, Mother, you so close, moving closer, and between us this speeding road with the arms of its orchards raised mutely on all sides.

Last night we spoke of your dead friends, your two sisters who have just left you, and then, recalled Daddy's words when I was born. "Now you have a daughter, and she will give you grandchildren, and after that, great grandchildren," all of which has come to pass…

The trees are unfruited and dusky green, their lower branches grazing the brown dance floor, their twiggy tops lifting their highest leaves toward the dizzying clouds. We are passing them fast, too fast to see what they are making as they drag hundreds of seeds all the way from the sun with their relentless silent effort.

Your Unbecoming

The urge
to not soil oneself
laid down during those precious
toddler months with smiles and coaxing
candy and books on the toilet seat
or stern looks and punishing glances…
What were the arts and wiles
threats and consequences?
And now that you are at a certain border
where it is all being brought into play
again and again and the night nurse (of course they
are understaffed here) cajoles sweetly with
an Ah, Honey, or says briskly with a cool glance,
"Don't you worry about it, just let yourself go."
How do you cross that particular border?
What do you find to say to yourself, no one
there to help you with your unbecoming?

And those two teeth on top, they're infected,
they'll just have to come out.

On the Dumping of Pianos

"To be honest with you, the guys enjoy it. They try
so hard all day not to scratch anything. And all of
a sudden they get to throw it off the truck."
—Brian Goodwin, piano mover
The New York Times, July 30. 2014

So, some of them land with their legs in the air
I am told, although I haven't seen it, some let out
a whole symphony of wailing, bang bang as
they are tossed and some get the axe, their dark
cabinets burned up for firewood. There is a huge
metal stove, too, that can demolish them, firebirds of
smoke billowing out, I imagine, Sviatoslav Richters
of heat melting their keys, curling their strings.

Thus, I wanted my mother's body watched from the moment
they tied the numbered tag around her white ankle
that I would never see again. I even signed papers
in advance for such a watcher, *shomer*, as he is called
in Hebrew, but when the time came, no one could be found
in the entire Coachella Valley, bang bang crash crash as
chord after chord went off in the darkened hospital room,
crash bang crash my fingers punching number after number on
my cell phone as she lay after her last *Shema* dressed in the gown
of red and pink flannel roses I had stitched by hand and her
grand-daughter had seamed with lime-green grosgrain ribbon.

The funeral home director thanked me for the pretty gown,
it being hard to sit in a room with someone else's mother
as he offered to do until I could return and relieve him,
bang crash the room so silent crash crash crash the baby grands,
the uprights, music stilled in them forever the *shomer* coming
at last down Highway 10 from L.A. with a pocket full of psalms

to relieve me late the next afternoon, my last sight of her in the light-
filled room, my last kiss over flannel and roses, not willing, not
able to ever imagine that kind of ruin for someone so upright,
so grand.

My Mom as Dylan Thomas

In those last afternoons
when all around her were hushing her back
against the sheets, peace, peace, they kept
saying she tried to leap from her bed and cried,
"Is there no out for me?"

"Fire them, fire them all," she said of the sweet
caregivers who just could not, would not take her
for one more walk, she, whose eye had not had enough
of seeing the green trees hung with yellow lemons
playing their little silver violins, and the palms waving
their majestic fans toward the snow-drizzled peaks
of the San Jacintos still bearing a little of that late
spring storm she had watched with awe and the humming
birds darting among the snapdragons, one of which stopped
to brood on a nest full of minuscule eggs each day my mom
as Dylan Thomas tried to drink herself back into life, tried to
snatch the whole bottle back from the small girl, smallest daughter
of the darkest night who whispered these final words to me,
"I'm thirsty. I want something to drink," before she curled herself
way back into her pillow and the baby hummingbirds hatched.

The Roadrunner

With a piece of something
dangling
from its beak
the roadrunner passed
your headstone, Mother,
and I'm sure did not see
the hand of your only son as it pulled the
blue silk coverings off and we stared
down at your carven name, the dates cut
so deeply in Hebrew and in Arabic the numerals,
one for the August day you came out of Grandma
one for the day in May you went back in

All the bird did was run
measuring with two toes forward
two toes backward
spring spring sprong
with its butch haircut
necking along measuring
an interval of grass and disturbing
for a few seconds what the rabbi
was intoning in her Kelly green-
plaid silk blouse, a tiny lace handkerchief
tucked mischievously into her breast
pocket, not like any rabbi I've ever seen
nor is the roadrunner, not even able to fly
much, ground cuckoo that it is, like any other bird…

Together they managed, though,
two spectacles that they were,
to mark the moment when all
you were to me
stood naked, carved in blue granite
against the grass for all to see.

Bye Bye Blackbird

In the last days you seemed younger, flamboyant,
dashing around the halls in your wheelchair
at the Desert Hospital in that cherry blossom
print kimono I found for you, with your favorite caregiver,
a young Filipino nurse who, after you were
deeply attached to him, suddenly left for a better job.

"Bye Bye Blackbird" you sang out, lips dark pink, eyes all blue
"Pack up all my cares and woes, Here I go, swingin' low,"
as you went inward, days, nights, "So, make my bed and light the light,
I'll arrive late tonight."

I couldn't see in, but could hear you, and all through the desert night
on your last ride you continued, passing cactus, passing sage, your last
instructions clear in my ear, "You're the one to be sure I look right
in the carriage, honey," all the way down Ramon Road. past
Date Palm Drive into Cathedral City where the cemetery lives,
stop lights, go lights, with a wave of your white-gloved hand,
a Liza Minnelli smile, black cane tucked under your armpit:
"I said Blackbird, Oh, Blackbird, Bye Bye…"

The Butterfly Blouse

There you are at Reouven's bar mitzvah in a translucent
blouse appliquéd in multicolored butterflies, long pearls hanging
over the black silk shell Amy stitched up for you right before we
flew

And here we are, all in one long printed line, great-grandson,
granddaughter, you, and me, your oldest daughter, the one writing
all of this down

You turned a dazzling smile toward the camera as you stood with
Reouven in that party hall in Paris where minutes later you and I
trudged through the sea of black-hatted men (seated separately from
the women, of course) to reach the one and only bathroom in the place

I know you wanted the perfect orthodox burial, Mother, the little white
shroud like a space suit all buttoned up, folded over you, and the white
bonnet tied just so

But at the last moment I had to send them to accompany you the bright,
winged ones trapped in their gauzy blouse straight from that last *simcha*

"Yes, it's done!" winked the attendant from Desert Memorial Park
used to many such bizarre requests

So that here I may sit years later among softly rustling trees and imagine
their wings carrying you breast heart shoulders flutter fluttering through
that sea of black hats

All the way home…

Acknowledgments

My appreciation to the editors of the following publications where some of these poems first appeared, sometimes in different versions:

"The Roadrunner," *Marin Poetry Center Anthology* (Volume XVII, 2014)

"On the Dumping of Pianos," *Marin Poetry Center Anthology* (Volume XVIII, 2015)

"Clair de Lune," *California Quarterly* (Summer, 2020, Volume 46, #2)

My grattitude to Laurel Feigenbaum and Judy Crowe who helped shape this manuscript; to Shawn Aveningo Sanders for choosing to publish, edit and design it; to my cover design consultants Susan Weissman and Amy Stock Drozd, as well as to Robert R. Sanders for the final cover design; and to Marcelo Holot for my author photo.

Praise for Bye Bye Blackbird

"In *Bye Bye Blackbird*, poet Doreen Stock leads us through a dark tempest where navigating a torrent of family matters, she witnesses with vivid imagery and an unflinching eye, the final strains of a mother who's lived a long, exuberant life.

—Michael D. Amitin, Parisian musician,
International Beat Poet Laureate, 2020-2021

"A medley of poems and prose-poems revealing with compassion, humor and musical remembrances the loving relationship between a daughter and her mother, in life and death. Of the poems I was particularly moved by the especial brilliance of "Mother Horse."

—Jack Hirschman, American poet & activist
and San Franciso Poet Laureate Emeritus

"Doreen Stock is a master of her craft, and her newest collection of poems captures her mother's last days and beyond with heart-wrenching grace, beauty, humanity, and artistry. Each poem is a jewel, a layered world of story, memory, love and senses, light and dark. Her work does what only the best art can: it connects readers with what it is to love, to lose, and to be fully alive in this world. You will keep this book on your shelf as a reminder of what matters, and you will want to come back to it again and again.

—Julie Fingersh, freelance journalist and writer,
The New York Times and *O: The Oprah Magazine*

About the Author

Fairfax, Californian poet, literary translator, and memoir practitioner, Doreen Stock, recently launched a chapbook of poems, *Tango Man*, (Finishing Line Press) in August 2020. Other works include: *My Name Is Y*, (Norfolk Press, 2019), an anti-nuclear memoir; *Three Tales from the Archives of Love*, (Norfolk Press, 2018), a work of historical fiction; *Talking with Marcelo*, (Mine Gallery Editions, 2017), a book-length interview of Argentine Journalist Marcelo Holot; *In Place of Me*, Poems Selected and with an Introduction by Jack Hirschman, (Mine Gallery Editions, 2015); *The Politics of Splendor*, (Alcatraz Editions, Santa Cruz, 1984), poems and translations. An interview and reading of Doreen's poetry can be viewed online at Marin Poet's Live! She is a founding member of The Marin Poetry Center.

Visit doreenstock.com or facebook.com/doreen.stock.52, for further information and current ruminations.

About The Poetry Box®

The Poetry Box® is a boutique publishing company in Portland, Oregon, who provides a platform for both established and emerging poets to share their words with the world through beautiful printed books and chapbooks.

Feel free to visit the online bookstore (thePoetryBox.com), where you'll find more titles including:

Matrimony by Laurel Feigenbaum

Nothing More to Lose by Carolyn Martin

Notes from a Caregiver by Meg Lindsay

Like the O in Hope by Jeanne Julian

A Shape of Sky by Cathy Cain

The Very Rich Hours by Gregory Loselle

Just the Girls by Pamela R. Anderson-Bartholet

Between States of Matter by Sherry Rind

The Kingdom of Birds by Joan Colby

Building a Woman by Deborah Meltvedt

My Mother Never Died Before by Marcia B. Loughran

Mouth Quill by Kaja Weeks

and more . . .

www.ingramcontent.com/pod-product-compliance
Ingram Content Group UK Ltd.
Pitfield, Milton Keynes, MK11 3LW, UK
UKHW022217230426
12048UKWH00016BA/906